Living Life While Loving God

Angel Moreira

ISBN:9781737927112

Angel Moreira Publishing: New York City, New York

CONTENTS

Part I: Living Life

A Prayer To The Lord 3
The Invisible Christian 5
Sinning And Not Winning 6
One Foot In And One Foot Out 8
Never Going To leave You Again 10
My Addiction 12
I'm The Way I Used To Be 13
Fornication 15
Adultery 16
I See You 17
I'm Coming Out 19
Drinking Excessively 21
One Day At A Time 23
Dealing With My Past 25
You Strengthen Me 27
Mysterious Ways 29
Faith Without Works 31
Faith Vs Fear 32
Work On Me For You 34
My Motivation 36
What's My Purpose 38
Finding Ways To Serve You 40
Stepping Up 42
My C.E.O 44
Idolizing Money 46
Trusting You 48
Waiting For Marriage 50
Celibacy 52
Celibacy Prayer 53
Pleasuring One Self 54
Being Judged 55

I'm Not Perfect 57

Lost Love 59

Losing An Angel 60

Heaven On Earth 61

Hell On Earth 62

Appreciation Prayer 63

Exposing My Enemy 64

Your Soldier 66

No Show 68

Late,Late,Late 69

Preach Pastor Preach 70

Failing But Trying 72

I'm Being Underestimated 74

Right On Time 76

Waiting On My Turn 78

Blessed To Be A Blessing 80

A Blessed Mindset 81

I'm Nothing Without You 83

Lazy Christian 85

Christian Crush 87

A Great Wife Prayer 89

A Great Husband Prayer 90

Finding Someone To Love 92

Testing Me 94

Praying Warrior 95

God Made 96

Not Hearing Your Voice 97

The Darkness 98

Dwelling In A Safe Place 100

Part II: Loving God

It's All About You 103

Thank You For Being You 104

Living Life While Loving You 106

PART I:
Living Life

A Prayer To The Lord

Lord, I come to
You
Broken and bruised,
Tired and used.

Misled and abused.

I ask you to
Strengthen me
From the pain that's
Ruining me.

My mind
My heart
My soul.

I need thy hands to
Take control.

Cover me with your love
And protect me from
This storm
Heal me, renew my mind so
I can reform.

And be the best I can be
For me and you as your
Servant
Because you truly

Deserve it.

Amen.

The Invisible Christian

Yes, I've been
Missing,
Lost in this world as a
Christian.

I have not been
Praying,
I haven't been going
To church
Or reading my Bible.

Or praising you with a Godly
Title.

I just been in this
World
Doing what I want to
Do
Without the acknowledgement
Of you.

However, I'm sorry
I never meant to hurt you
Or be someone that's invisible.

Sinning And Not Winning

Sinning is only good for
A season,
Granting you satisfaction
That's appeasing.

However, it's
Temporary
While placing our God
Secondary.

It may be complicated to
Stop sinning because we are
Only human
And brought into this world from humans
That has fallen.

And it's in our nature
To desire
The pleasures of this
World.

The dark pleasures in
Life.

However, if we are doing
Wrong,
We are not doing what's
Right.

We have to blow away sinning
As if it was the wind from a
Fan.

Due to the fact that when we are sinning,
We are not winning
This is something we have to
Understand.

One Foot In And
One Foot Out

I'm stuck in a
Place
That's in a peculiar
Space.

As if I have two
Faces
Going through dark and
Light phases.

Some of the things I do, you would
Approve
Other things I do, you may ask "what is going on
With you?"

I'm trying to completely be in
The spiritual world
And not be a product of this
World.

But temptations have me so
Weak
It's something I must
Defeat.

So I can grow
Mentally
As well as
Spiritually.

Because you are the only
Way.

And there's no other
Route
However, momentarily, I have one foot in
And one foot out.

Never Going To Leave
You Again

I don't know
Why
I became
Distant.

And now that I'm back
With you,
I think about it every
Minute.

I was just out
There
Without a
Care,

Overlooking you without
Any fear,

Just doing
Me
And I know you are disappointed
Deeply.

But I'm here now,
Broken,
Arriving so humbly.

And thank you.

For accepting
Me.

But this time Lord,
I'm not going to leave.

My Addiction

I've been
Using,
And the body that's my temple,
I've been abusing.

I want to stop
My addiction
And move forward with
My mission.

My mission to focus
On you and serve you.

Despite being held
Back
From something that's taking
Me off track,

I'm ready to let
Go
And grow
And become more of the person you
Love and know.

I'm Not The Way I Used To Be

I'm not at the spiritual level
I want to be,
But I'm not the way I used to
Be.

Sometimes I come across
Temptation and face defeat,
But I'm not the way I used to
Be.

Every now and then, the tone of
My voice can be so harsh, and I can be rude,
But I've changed my attitude,
I'm not the way I used to be.

When celebrating a special occasion
Over dinner
I may have a little too much
Liquor,
But I'm not the way I used to be.

Sometimes I still judge and criticize
Others,
But what I've discovered
Is that I'm not the way I used to
Be.

I forget to love thy neighbor as sisters and
Brothers,

But I'm not the way I used to be.

I'm getting better and growing in
Christ
Others and I can see it in
Me
It's all because of you and
I'm not the way I used to be.

Fornication

Lord, I know I didn't take an
Oath and Martial vows,
But I'm naked in these sheets some
How.

I mean I know why,
And I can't lie
Or deny
These sexual urges I have
Inside.

I'm supposed to wait until I'm
Married,

But I'm failing
Drastically
I have to make some changes
In order for you to receive the results
I need
This is something I will
Work on correcting
Day to day
Please give me the strength to over come
My weakness.

And put an end
To committing Fornication.

Adultery

I have my
Husband or Wife,
But I feel like I need someone
Different in my life.

I always want to step
Outside
From what I have
Inside.

But this lie,
This sin
Will destroy me
Within.

I don't know what to
Do
I've been praying and trying,
But I'm still acting like a fool.

I have the love of my
Life
And someone I don't want to
Lose.

Because the selfishness
In me
I want to put an end to
Committing Adultery.

I See You

When I was hurt
And my heart was broken,
You were there for me and
That's for certain.

Lord, I see you.

When I didn't have any
Money
And I was trying to make it day to
Day,
You came and made a way.

Lord, I see you.

When my health was down
And I was sick,
With the help of your angels,
You've cured it.

Lord, I see you.

When I was lost and couldn't
Be found,
You stepped in
And gave me direction with your
Godly crown.

Lord, I see you.

When people tried to tear me down
And hurt me,
You were my protection, placing your
Fence around me.

Lord, I see you.

And I appreciate, praise and acknowledge
All the things you do.

Lord, I see you.

I'm Coming Out

I'm in this
Ditch
Stuck in the trenches,
But I hear your voice as
I listen.

I'm coming out.

I'm drowning at the
Bottom of the ocean,
But as I kick my feet
And move my hands,
I'm elevating while strengthening my
Motion.

I'm coming out.

I'm in this dark
Tunnel
I can't see anything,

Anywhere
Wait, I see a glare
Hitting my eyes,
And I see a light that's near
I'm coming out
My heart is filled with pain, hurt
And so many emotions
Because of the storms in
Life.

Then this calm peace came over me,

Causing me to feel
Alright.

That can only be you Lord.

I'm coming out.

Drinking Excessively

There's something I've been
Dealing with;
It's a quick
Fix.

Well, at least that's how I
Perceive it.

A coping mechanism that's
Toxic.

It allows me to
Relax
And escape my
Pain
However, it leads me to other
Detrimental things.

That cause problems in my
Life
That darkness that push me away
From the light.

I want to give drinking
Up
Because I've had
Enough.

So with rehab, prayer, faith, and a strong
Mind over matter,
I'm going to focus on climbing out of this
While becoming better after.

After this phase of my
Life,
I see a better tomorrow in my
Sight
So I can grow in Christ and be a better
Me.

Lord, I'm going to put an end to drinking
Excessively.

One Day At A Time

Right now, all I can
Do
Is focus on
You.

And take it one day
At a time.

Instead of looking
Down,
I'm going to lift my head up
As I walk around.

And take it one day
At a time.

I'm going to move forward
With faith
While putting a smile on my
Face.

And take it one day
At a time.

I'm not going to worry
And keep my mind at peace
Because I know that you are here
For me
And no one can be against me
So there's no need for anything

As I take it one day
At a time.

Dealing With My Past

I think of my past
Drama;
The pain I've felt
And trauma.

I've prayed
To heal
However, at times the
Pain is something I still feel.

I try to move
Forward
But the memories
Still remain in my mind.

Knowing my pain will heal
With prayer and time
And after the rainy
Days, the sun will shine.

I'm blessed
To be out of any mess.

With a testimony
From a test,
Experiencing many
Blessings
After harsh life
Lessons,

I know you are
Beside me.

Even when I'm
Hurting.

But somehow, the pain
Resides in me
Despite the fact that you've
Been here with me.

I just hope the pain and thoughts
No longer last
And I find complete joy because
I'm still dealing with my past.

You Strengthen Me

At one point in my life,
I was devastated,
Confused, crippled, ran over, broke
And humiliated.

The water from my eyes
Wouldn't stop
With severe pain in my
Heart
While I fell
Apart.

I didn't know if I should
Go right or left;
Everything was
Disarrayed.

But I looked for answers
Within you.

And now, I'm standing
Tall
I don't feel that pain
Anymore.

My spirit is well and
Alive
Lord, I feel so good
Inside.

Your love have me higher
Than any other high.

You came to restore
Me
Thank you for picking me up
When I was weak
Thank you for strengthening me.

Mysterious Ways

Lord, I may not know
Why certain unfortunate things happen
To me,
But I know one thing;
I know you want the best for me.

And when I'm in
The dark,
You allow me to
See.

You break me down to
The floor
So you can build me up
Better than I've been before.

Or you may close certain
Doors
Because you have something
Better in store.

It's not always about
What I think I need,
It's about what you have for
Me
So even when I'm confused
And I don't know what to do,

I know that
I will be okay.

Because you work in
Mysterious ways.

Faith Without Works

Lord, I find myself
Praying,
Then I start
Worrying.

I always say I'm going
To put it in your hands
However, following that I
Do what I can.

To make things
Right
While adding stress to my
Life,

Which eliminate me from
Having a peace of mind,

I have to truly
Give it to you
And trust the process as
You and I move.

Because you are the glory
And the head
And I understand that faith without
Works is dead.

Faith Vs Fear

Having a vision to do
Things for you
Isn't enough, I have
To bring it to life too.

I see the vision in
My mind
And I want to bring things to
Life for you in time.

But I also feel worried
I feel worried about falling short
And missing the shot as if I was playing
On a basketball court.

And I think about
The interference of Satan
And negative people
Hating.

Despite the fact I
Can do all things through Christ who
Strengthens me,
Sometimes I still
Worry.

I'm battling between
Faith and fear,
But with having faith,
I should not feel fear
Anywhere.

So I have to build on
Faith
And triumph over
Fear.

Because worrying and having fear
Will not allow me to get anywhere.

Work On Me For You

Sometimes in life,
I selfishly think about me
Instead of focusing on
You.

Or I feel like I should
Do things one way
Without considering your
Way.

Or sometimes I don't
Do certain things for you because of
Fear
Or I'll procrastinate and it would
Take me about a year
Just to get things going
With excuse after excuse leading to
No results showing.

However, I have to overcome
My fears and doubts
And my negative self-talk that I
Can live without.

I also have to overcome
My shortcomings and sins;
It's an ongoing battle I have to
Win
I struggle sometimes but I'll rely in
The power I have in you within.

Sometimes I tell myself

It's okay because you know my
Heart
But a deceptive mentality is something
I should have put an end to before it starts.

I just ask you lord to
Work in me for you
As I work on me for you
You've created me for you so I can do the
Things you've called me to do.

My Motivation

I'm at a place
In life
That if it's not for you,
It's not right.

I want to push
For you
And be the best for
You.

I'm trying to align
My ways
As I spread the word
With faith.

It's not always
Easy,
And I also struggle
As a human being.

However, as an imperfect
Being,
I push toward doing
Things.

Things for
Christ
And focus on you
With my life.

And trying to be
A light.

A light for you Lord
A light for
Christ.

What's My Purpose

Lord, I'm trying
To understand
What's in your
Plan.

What's destined
For me
And what do you
Need?

I will serve
You
But I'm not sure on what
You want me to do.

I recognize some of
My gifts,
And I try to focus on you
With it.

I guess I have to be
Patient.

Can you give me
A sign
To let me know that I'm
Going the right way?

Because it's so much
Confusion day to day.

Despite the fact it can be
Satan working in me,
Trying to redirect
Me,
So many road blocks, obstacles
And curses,
Can you just guide me
To my purpose?

**Finding Ways To
Serve You**

Lord, I'm thinking of ways
To serve you
With the things I can
Do.

Despite the fact that the decision
Is on you,

I have certain weakness
And certain strengths.
I will work on my weakness
Within.

So I can combine the
Two and begin.

I will spread your
Word
The best way I
Can.

Whether it's visually, vocally
Or written,
But at this moment, you only
Know where it ends.

Because I only have ideas
Of what I can do.

Ideas and thoughts
To serve you.

Stepping Up

I usually sit back and
Observe,
Watch the preacher preach
The word.

Sunday is the main
Day,
I'm not involved in any
Way.

However, I can give more
To you
With the things I
Do.

You've blessed me with
Gifts
That I can serve you
With.

I'm ready to step
Up,
And hiding behind the scene,
I'm ready to give up.

It's all about
You
When it comes to
Me.

Therefore, I ask you to
Enlighten me,

So I can work for you
Completely.

My C.E.O

I have this business idea
In my mind,
But can you help me with the vision
Just in case my eyes are blind
Give me the wisdom
To make the right decisions
And the insight to grow the
Business.

That will be
So helpful
In addition, it
Represents you.

That's all I
Need;
You as the head,
Commander and chief.

Guide me as I
Move

And build a business
That's profitable.

To where people can
See you and want to
Serve you with the things
They do.

I will be here working
Diligently.

When things are going well
And when things are harder,
Because I have you as the C.E.O,
My God and father.

Idolizing Money

Sometimes we make money
Our number one priority
Whether it's consciously or
Unconsciously.

And we say things like,
I have to get this money,
I'm trying to get my money
Right
Without truly accepting that you
Are the reason for the things we
Have in our life.

And only a few of us
May say
I have to get right with
You
I'm trying to be better for
You
I'm trying to correct my
Walk for you with the things
I do.

Most of us mainly focus
On money.

Money over
Everything,
Some people will
Say.

Or secure the B or get

To The B
The B is for the bag
And not the Bible,
Unfortunately,
Respectfully.

Yes we need
Money
However, we need you more
Than anything.

And sometimes we treat others
Without money unfairly and funny.

We prefer not to associate with
People who don't have much

Or people dealing with
Times that's tough.

Money is necessary
But you should always come first
And not secondary.

Trusting You

Every day, I feel like
I'm fighting for my life,
But I know you will make
Things right.

Every time I take a step
Forward,
It end up being two steps
Backwards.

But I know that you
Are okay with that,
I know you allow
Setbacks.

So you can make
Things better
And you will keep things
Together.

As I go through
These tribulations and trials,
I will pray with joy and try to continue
To push for miles.

Due to the fact that I have
You with me
And that's all I really
Need,

All I can
Do

Is put my trust in you.

Waiting For Marriage

I'm going to
Wait
Until I walk
Down the aisle
Because I know it will make
You smile.

I will give myself
To you
Before I say
I do.

To someone with a love
That's true.

I will stay a
V
Until you send
Who's for me.

I will focus on remaining
A virgin that's
Pure
While focusing on what you
Placed me here on earth for.

Even when it get rough
And I get weak,
I will get on my
Knees.

And pray for the strength to
Overcome my flesh and temptation
And avoid sexual relations.

I will try my best
And wait
Until after that special wedding
Day.

Celibacy

I know I'm hot
And I'm in so much heat,
I'm trying to diminish
The sexual urges within me,

But I happen to be
A freak
And I feel so
Weak.

I'm trying to live the
Way I should
It's hard because I want
Someone to make me feel good.

I haven't had sexual
Intercourse in a while.

I have to sustain myself
Somehow
And deny myself
From something going down.

I'm trying to grow
Spiritually
But lust for the flesh
Is tempting me
While practicing celibacy.

Celibacy Prayer

Lord, I'm having a
Moment
My sexual urges always
Surface.

I can't help myself
Looking at the opposite sex,
Then thinking to myself "while
You know what else is next".

I've been doing
Fine
But I always have sex on
My mind.

I think I need to take a long cold
Shower
Please give me the
Power.

And the discipline.

To live my life free
From sexual sin.

Pleasuring One Self

Trying to walk the walk
In every way can be challenging,
And living without pleasure is something
One may be battling.

Having sex out of wedlock is
A sin
But sex is something one may desire
As a human.

Therefore, one may result to
Pleasing oneself
While fantasizing about someone
Else.

And looking at videos and images
Filled with lust
Due to restraining themselves from
Being with someone else physically,
Which can be tough.

In addition, it can lead one to falling then attempting
To get up
Or putting one in a place where one may
Need help
By pleasuring oneself excessively
While keeping things away from everyone else.

However, what one can do is pray,
Read the word, or seek counsel
And allow the spirit to overcome the flesh
Which can put pleasuring oneself to rest.

Being Judged

Because I'm living for
You
I'm under a magnify glass
With the things I do.

It can be very
Challenging
And it can also
Be disappointing.

Because I'm capable of
Making mistakes,
I can't do anything that's
Not aligned with you.

People look at me
In a negative way.

What hurt the most
Is that it can come from
Other believers as well
Some of them be ready
To send me to hell.

And act as if they don't sin
As well.

People that are not
Christians judge,
Then they use it as a reason
To not praise you
And seek your love.

I'm not sure on what they
Are thinking of.

It can be very
Hard
But I know you are the
Only person who can judge me
God.

I'm Not Perfect

Sometimes I have a vision of being
A perfect Christian
Then I continue with life and thoughts
Of sinning begin.

Then I realize
That I'm not perfect.

I could be on the right
Track
Doing things right,
Then I'll have a set
Back.

This makes me
Realize
That I'm not
Perfect.

I'm putting forth
The effort and looking
For the day.

That I can live by the word
In every way
From my mind, spirit, actions
And everything I say.

I will focus on being my
Best and nothing less.

And when it happens,

My sins, I will be able
To correct.

I will be the best I can be
But I will not be perfect.

Lost Love

I know someone who
Was close to me
But now it's someone I no
Longer see.

We had our differences
And fell apart
But I can still feel them in
My heart.

I also feel as if they were
In the dark.

Hiding secrets and doing
Things that's not of your light
Can you just save their soul
As they continue with life?

I feel like they were too intrigued
With worldly things
And focusing on Satan
Dreams.

As if their soul was asked to be
Sacrificed,
Can you protect their
Life?

Losing An Angel

I received some
News
That's very sad and
Hurtful.

I guess you've decided
To take one of your Angels from
Earth
I know they're in a better
Place but it hurts.

You took someone who's genuine
And loved unselfishly,
A great soul for
Humanity.

But it was their
Time.

They will be
Missed
Despite wishing things were
Different,
They are with you,
Which is great, but it's something
I'm trying to handle
And I'm going to try to smile after losing
An Angel.

Heaven On Earth

Waking up is better than my
Best dream
As I serve you, operating in
The fruit of the spirit or high
Vibrational frequency,

My fantasy
Is my reality
And I've found
Peace emotionally.

I have heaven in
My soul
Because of
You,
While I appreciate what
You've given me in this
World with abundance
Of gratitude.

You are my
Source
You are my
Reason
For being.

My light and everything
It's worth,
And you are the reason
For me feeling like I'm in heaven
On earth.

Hell On Earth

Lord, the pain inside
Of me
Burns deep as if it was
One thousand degrees.

I feel as if I'm under
Attack
And satan is on my
Back.

Trying to destroy
My soul,
And he has a firm
Grip without trying to let go,

Coming for my spirit
In multiple directions
With all his aggression.

If I didn't know
You,

I would feel like I'm
Cursed
Because it feels like I'm in hell on earth.

Apprecation Prayer

At times I find myself
Praying for the things I want
And need
Without truly appreciating
My blessings.

I pray for the things
I don't have
But today, I want to focus on
The things I have.

Lord,

Thank you
For life
Thank you for
Making my wrongs
Right and
Thank you for loving
Me in every way
Thank you for providing
Me with what
I need
Day to day
Thank you for
Accepting me
And thank for being
My everything.

Exposing My Enemy

Satan was once an angel
In heaven,
And even though he was
An angel,
His intention was not of the
Light.

Lord, it's the same way with
People in life.

They act as if they are here
For me
But they only end up hurting
Me.

Sometimes they will smile
In my face,
Knowing the acts of their wicked
Ways.

With the intent of betraying
Me,
With the intent to use
Me,
With the intent to abuse
Me.

Acting as if they are truly
Here for me.

Acting as if they care
For me.

But through it all,
You find a way to show me
That some people are not
Here for me.

And I want to thank you
For exposing my enemy.

Your Soldier

Because I have a
Mission,
Satan pays extra
Attention.

He knows you have
Amazing things for me
However, he does not want them
To be achieved.

I know everything will not
Be laid out like a red carpet;
Satan is going to try to stop
It.

It's like a spiritual warfare on
Earth,
And there will be pain, disappointment
And hurt.

But I'm ready;

I'm ready to
Fight
And serve in
Christ.

Despite what the enemy may bring
My way,
I'm equipped with your favor at
The end of the day
Because I'm your soldier,

I wish he knew the fight is
Already fixed,
And when everything is over and
Done, I already win.

No Show

It's Sunday morning
However, I'm not in church
Today
I was unable to find
A way.

But I still found the strength to
Pray.

And talk to
You
About all the things
I've been going through.

I wanted to
Go
And I needed to
Go.

My emotions and pain
Overwhelmed me
Even though I'm truly in
Need.

In need of the
Word,
But I will open my Bible
And I guess this time,
I can watch service
Online.

Late Late Late

Every Sunday morning,
I find myself
Being late, and Lord,
I need help.

Honestly,

At times I'm late
Purposely.

However, there are
Many times
When I want to be on
Time
But when I'm home
Getting ready, I lose track
Of time.

This is a problem
That I'm facing,
But I will put forth
The effort and keep praying.

I will trust in myself
And have faith

And I will stop being so
Late.

Preach Pastor Preach

God is with you as you
Preach
There are so many souls you
Are healing and you've reached.

I can feel the spirit
In the church
As you preach the
Word.

The way you break
Things down,
It's so clear, understanding
And profound.

As you mention that you
Don't know who you are talking
To today,
I'm one of the members
That you are speaking to in every
Way.

And let the church say
Amen and praise.

As you
Preach,
I can feel it in
My soul and my
Feet.

Because your service is incredible

And unforgettable.

Preach pastor
Preach.

Failing But Trying

In some areas, I'm doing
Great, and I'm getting better
But with other things, I really
Need to get it together.

I'm trying
But it's not enough
I have to try harder with
The support of your love.

Yes, I've failed the
Test
When it comes to
Lusting for the flesh

Or I find myself
Consistently thinking
About drinking.

I want to stop using drugs
However, it's the only thing
I think of.

And sometimes my
Attitude
Can be very cruel.

I also still find myself

Being selfish
Instead of being selfless.

I also can't forget
About missing church.

As if waking up on
Sunday mornings hurts.

I'm trying
But I find myself
Lying

And failing
Again, again, and
Again
But for you, lord I will
Keep on trying.

I'm Being Underestimated

People look at me
And doubt the things I can
Do
Without acknowledging that
I have you.

They will watch me
Fall,
Then think I will not
Succeed at all.

And I may get over looked
From the short comings they
See
They act as if I don't
Have you lord with me.

And it may not look like
I'm winning
But this is just the
Beginning.

Once you are ready to send
Your blessings
Down from heaven,
They will know it's from you
Without a question.

When it's time to lift
Me,

It will be an amazing
Sight to see.

Right On Time

Sometimes I pray for things
And expect it right away
Within the time frame of a
Few months to a couple of days.

But I realized that
My time
Is not always your
Time,
And your time is the right
Time.

Sometimes you may want
Me to grow
And learn new
Things,
Or you may feel like
I'm not ready.

You may want me
To learn a life lesson
Before the blessing.

I'm becoming more
Understanding of that
Which brings more awareness
To my mind.

At times things don't happen
In my time.

It happens
In your time,
The right time.

Waiting On My Turn

You are the reason for
Blessings
Without any second
Guessing.

All the glorious
And wonderful things
You do,
Causing many dreams
To come true
To where it's undeniable
And unstoppable.

I've seen how you've
Blessed many
How you took people from
Scarcity to plenty.

I've watched how you
Raise people from the bottom
To the top
And take them from cold to
Hot.

And what you've done
For them,
You can do for me.

So I will wait here
Patiently
As you work in me,
On me and around me.

I'm preparing and waiting
For my next blessings.

Blessed To Be A Blessing

I know that you have
Blessed me
So I can be a
Blessing.

A blessing to
Others
And help build my
Sisters and brothers.

My sisters and brothers
In Christ
And improve others'
Lives.

What's given to
Me,
It's not just for
Me.

It's for others in
Need,

And I'm blessed
To be a blessing.

A Blessed Mindset

Sometimes I make the mistake
Of only looking at money, relationships and luxious
Things
As blessings.

Like a new job, business, spouse, cloths, jewelry, car
Or a house
Which narrows my perspective of blessings without
A doubt.

God has blessed me with some of these
Things
However, it's more to being blessed with his
Blessings.

I woke up this morning,
I'm blessed
My eyes opened today,
I'm blessed
I can still breathe,
I'm blessed
I have food to eat,
I'm blessed
I have clothing on my back
I'm blessed
I'm loved from a spouse, family
Or friend,
I'm blessed
I have a first and last name,
I'm blessed
I have shelter,
I'm blessed.

And I have security because I'm a child of God,
I'm blessed.

I'm blessed
Even when it look like things
Are a mess
Or when I'm going through a test,
Because I have God
And I'm blessed to have a blessed mindset.

I'm Nothing Without You

I could achieve
All my dreams
And do amazing
Things.

But I'm nothing without
You.

The world could perceive
Me as an image that is larger
Than life
As my dreams take
Flight.

But I'm nothing
Without you.

I may have amazing
Talents
But you are the reason
For it.

And I'm nothing without
You.

You are the reason
For my being
And the purpose
For the things I
Do.

And I'm nothing without
You.

Lazy Christian

Honestly,
I find myself
Being lazy.

Instead of
Reading the word,
I prefer to get the
Word.

Instead of reading the
Bible myself,
I prefer to get the Pastor's
Help.

In addition, when it
Comes to partaking in
Church activities,
I'm nowhere to be
Seen.

I can do
More
For you God,
It's not that
Hard.

I need to raise
Up
And be more
Active.

So I can accomplish

Your mission,
And I need to stop
Being a lazy Christian.

Church Crush

I'm trying to get
Things right
So I can serve you with my
Life.

I'm trying to become more of
You and improve,
But when attending church, I have
My eyes on someone so fine and beautiful.

I'm trying to praise
Your name,
But I can't help but to
Look their way,
And I'm not sure on what to do
Or say.

I'm not sure if I should
Make a move
Because I'm supposed to be
Praising you.

I came for healing
And manifestation.

However, the sight
Of them cause me
To lose my concentration.

I'm attending church to find
You
But when entering church,

Guess what I do?

I check for their attendance,
Then I praise you.

I know my priorities are
Screwed up
I have to get it together
However, I have a church crush.

A Great Wife Prayer

Lord, work on
Me,
Allow me to be a
Blessing.

A virtuous woman
That brings peace;
Peace to my husband
To be
Allow me to be loving,

Kind and nurturing,
Selfless, loyal and understanding.

And value a heart that's
Focused on you and not material things
A Godly heart that's loving and
Caring.

Allow me to be a safe
Space
That brings hope, encouragement,
Inspiration and faith.

Allow me to be a helpmate
While being an addition to someone's happiness
And I pray that I can be a wonderful wife to my
Future husband.

A Great Husband Prayer

I pray you work
On me
So I can be the best
Husband I can for
My wife to be.

A marriage is a journey
In life
That may not always be
Easy.

I pray that I can
Provide and protect with security.

I pray that I
Can compromise
When conflicts
Arise.

I pray I can be
Healthy to her
Soul
And love her with a heart
Of gold
I pray that I
Can be an asset
And not a
Liability
And love her
Faithfully
While standing by
Our Martial vows

Of for better or for worst,
In sickness or in health.

For the good and unfortunate times in life,
I pray I can be an amazing
Husband to my future wife.

Finding Someone To Love

I know what I
Want
However, I'm not sure if
What I want is what you
Want for me.

Or what I
Want
Is the person I
Need.

I question if I
Should rearrange
My list
Or have it dismissed.

I know you have someone
For me
Even though I've been
Failing.

Failing to find
Love,
Failing to find someone
Special.

Failing to maintain
A bond
That's unbreakable and
Strong.

I focused on what I

Wanted physically
And not spiritually.

However, sometimes I
May feel like someone is what I
Want spiritually, but they are
Deceiving,
Acting without
Being.

I just have to trust the process
While focusing on bettering me as I focus on you,
And eventually, I'll meet the one for me too.

Testing Me

I'm trying to be
A good civilized human
However, people want to test me
To where they can get these hands.

Lord, please continue to guide
Me
Because I know you don't want
Me out here like a G.

At times people can be so
Disrespectful and rude,
As if they can't get
Handled.

However, I know you represent
Love and peace
Humility, humbleness and meekness
Is what you seek.

Even though I'm being tested
In these streets,
I ask you to allow me to be more of you
And less of me.

Praying Warrior

Life has many
Battles
And many issues
To tackle.

But when I'm being
Attacked
By the enemy,
I have to be prepared
For all things.

So if I feel unsure
Or scared,
I get on my knees and
Say a prayer.

When trouble arise and
Things get hard,
I call on you God.

And when I'm confused

And don't know what
To do,
I call on you
To help me with my
Battles.

God Made

Sometimes people want to know
How I do the things I do,
How I move the way I
Move.

They may say it's something
Different about you;

Your ways are
Different
Your style is
Different.

You are always
Winning
Even if you are not
Winning.

How did you get
To be the way you
Are
With a light inside and outside of you that
Shines like a
Star,

That radiate day
To day?

All I can say is, "I'm God made".

Not Hearing Your Voice

At times I hear others
Say
What they've heard from you
And the things you say.

I think that's amazing
And great
However, at this moment, I
Don't feel that way.

At times I feel like you
Want me to do things a certain
Way
But the sound of your voice
Seems so far away.

I'm assuming I have to grow
Spiritually and change some of
My sinful ways.

Then I'll get the wonderful
Opportunity of hearing your
Voice someday.

The Darkness

The world has become
So dark,
And it's so much pain
And sadness in our hearts.

Wickedness in high places
In different stages
Division amongst humans
From different races.

Human suffering upon us
Without hesitation,
Living life as if we are in the book
Of Revelations.

It's heartbreaking to see
The world we live in and
The truth we are facing

We know it's
Written
But now it's truly
The world we live in.

We came to a place
Where the world lost so much
Compassion,

And hearts are filled with
Hardness.

But we will look to the
Light with hope
As we transition out of the
Darkness.

Dwelling In A Safe Place

In a world of destruction
And chaos,
My soul
And heart break.

Death, control and suffering
Are infectious
However, I have you as my
Protection.

Some people are
Uncertain
And wildly
Running
But I have you for
My covering

Covering me like
A shield
As Satan try to destroy
And kill.

Kill and eradicate
However, I dwell in a safe
Place.

PART II:
LOVING GOD

It's All About You

As I thankfully
Wake up in a blessed way,
Do you need anything from
Me today?

Even though I may not always
Understand you at times
And all the things you
Say,
I'm here for you
I'm here for you in
Every way.

Just let me
Know
Because I'm ready to
Go.

I'm ready to be
On the move.

And do the things
You want me to do.

Because when it comes
To me,
I want everything to be about
You.

Thank You For Being You

Thank you for being
So magnificent
Thank you for being
So amazing.

Thank you for forgiving us
For our sins
Thank you for being
So loving.

Thank you for showing me
The light.

Thank you being there for me
In life.

Thank you for your
Mercy
Thank you for blessing
Me
And being everything.

Thank you for giving
Hope
Thank you for your
Faith.

Thank you for answering me
When I pray
Thank for all the amazing things
You do.

Thank you
Thank you for being you.

Living Life While Loving You

Living in this
World,
I will focus on you and
Not being of this world

It's a
Privilege
And I'm honored to give my soul
To you with the life
I'm living.

Even though at times it
Can be challenging
And I still get
Tempted,

Tempted by lust, sex, drinking,
Drugs or other things,

Living day to day,
Trying to overcome sinning,

But you gave your only son
For our sins
While forgiving us and positioning
Us to win.

And no one in this world can
Love me like you
Therefore, I give my heart, my
Soul and all of me to you.

QUOTES

God is not like people.

In life, when God calls you all you have to
do is answer.

Sometimes God will break you down so
he can reconstruct and rebuild you
into his divine masterpiece.

Knowing that God will use your pain for his
purpose in life is a blessing.

Believing that the light of God can bring
you out the darkness in life is a blessing.

In the journey of finding love, I focus
on God first.

Being able to recognize and appreciate your blessings
in life is a blessing.

Knowing when to forgive yourself and correct
yourself is a blessing.

At times in life as humans, we underestimate our gifts and God-given talents.

Having the ability to realize that God loves you is a blessing.

Sometimes in life as children of God, we make the mistake of valuing money more than our creator.

Having the ability to realize that God blesses his children is a blessing. So be blessed.

In life, when people count you out, count on God and count your blessings.

One of the best things you can do for yourself is to love God while living life.

Acknowledgements

I want to thank God and you for showing your support.

About The Author

Angel Moreira was born in New York City. He attended and graduated from Southwood High School in Shreveport, Louisiana. He has written Expressions Of The Heart, Expressions OF The Heart (The Second Edition), The Principles For Loving A Man (What Women Need To Know) along with R.J Chaney, and L.I.F.E (Living.Inspired.Free.Excelling). In addition, he's written and produced short screenplays, such as The Transition, The Recovery, and Model Life. Currently, he's working on his first full-length screenplay.

www.ingramcontent.com/pod-product-compliance
Lightning Source LLC
LaVergne TN
LVHW091310080426
835510LV00007B/450